ABOUT THE AUTHOR

Daniel Cohen was for many years the managing editor of *Science Digest* and is now a free-lance science writer. He has written numerous science articles for magazines as well as over a dozen books for children and adults. He has taught at the New School for Social Research.

ABOUT THE BOOK

Many people who look at pictures of the Great Pyramid of Egypt, Stonehenge in England, or other ancient monuments wonder how they were built. It seems incredible that people with the simplest of tools could have built such gigantic structures. Yet they did.
In clear, straightforward terms, this book explains how seven of the most celebrated ancient monuments were built. Examples are drawn from all parts of the world and from different historical periods. The book will give the reader a new understanding and appreciation of the accomplishments of technologically primitive peoples.

ABOUT THE ARTIST

Judith Gwyn Brown, a native New Yorker, graduated from New York University with a major in fine arts history. She has illustrated twenty-five books for children including *The Stone of Victory* and *The Grandma and The Apple Tree*. She is also an author of picture books. Miss Brown, who likes to travel, has visited Stonehenge.

ANCIENT MONUMENTS

And How They Were Built

By
Daniel Cohen

Drawings by
Judith Gwyn Brown

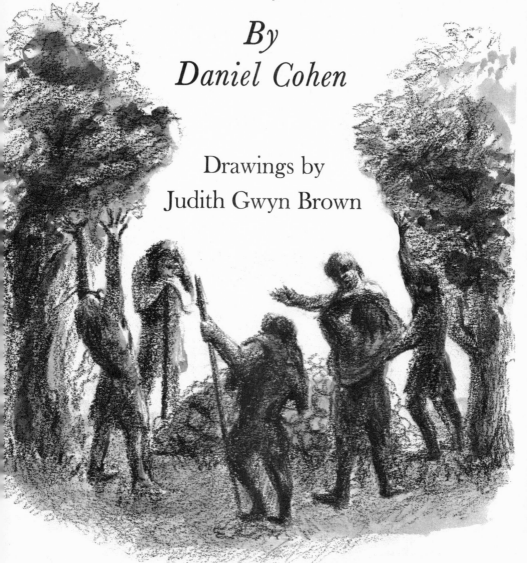

McGRAW-HILL BOOK COMPANY

New York · St. Louis · San Francisco
Montreal · Panama · Toronto

TO BUCK HARRIS

CONTENTS

I
MONUMENTS THEN AND NOW

THIS IS HOW monument building may have begun.

Thousands of years ago, long before people were organized into nations, and long before the first city was built, men lived in little groups. Those who depended upon hunting lived in small bands which followed the game from place to place. Those who planted crops had to stay in one place, so they lived in small villages. They owned practically nothing. The richest man, like the poorest, lived in a windowless hut of mud and leaves.

In one of these villages the head of the clan had died. He had lived for over fifty summers, and was a very old man by the standards of the time. Death was common in the village, and the old man's death came as no surprise. But he had been a good leader, and a wise one. He would be badly missed.

The villagers prepared for his funeral with unusual care. The body was painted with a red substance to give the pale flesh a rosy and more lifelike appearance. The corpse was then wrapped in a cloak made of animal skins and laid in a deep grave pit. A few tools and some jugs of grain and beer, which might be useful to the old man in his journey to the next world, were put in the grave with him. The appropriate spells were then recited, and the grave was filled in.

All had been done according to long-established custom. But somehow it did not seem like enough. In just a few years the grass and bushes would grow over the grave, and no one would remember where it had been. One day even the old man's name and many deeds would slowly be forgotten.

The villagers had no clear idea of what happened to a man after he died. They suspected that his spirit lived on in some fashion, and that the next world was very like this one. They also believed that the worlds of the living and the dead were connected, and that the dead drew strength from the living. If the living no longer remembered a dead man then his spirit might disappear. Then he truly would be dead and gone.

The people began to gather stones and pile them on top of the grave. It took a lot of work, but they finally heaped up a large mound of stones. The spot at which the old man was buried would not now be easily forgotten. The mound would serve as a reminder that underneath it lay a good and wise man. Perhaps the mound would give the dead man immortality.

This same sort of thing was happening in other parts of the world. Where there were no stones people used piles of bricks, made from dried mud. In other places they used piles of logs, or they simply piled up heaps of earth.

Of course, we cannot be sure that monument building began in this way. What we do know is that thousands of years ago many different peoples began to build large grave mounds. Some were so large that they must have taken a long time to build. Since life was hard for people thousands of years ago they had little time to spare, so that the mounds must have meant a great deal to them.

Later peoples began to build more elaborate tombs for their dead. They also began to build other sorts of monuments, temples, statues, fortresses, even cities. Anything that is larger and more elaborate than it has to be for practical purposes, can be considered a monument. Monument building became very important to people. By building something huge the builders could show the world how powerful they were, and ensure that in future times men would remember them long after they died.

It would be wrong to think that the age of monument building is over. We are still building plenty of monuments today, although we often do not call them that.

As this is being written the tallest building in the world is going up in New York City. The building is called the World Trade Center. When it is completed it will have two towers, each 104 stories high.

The World Trade Center will be an office building. But there are no practical reasons for making an office building that tall. Perfectly good offices can be provided more cheaply in much smaller buildings. Buildings like the World Trade Center are not built for practical reasons. They are built because the builders want to show what they can accomplish. Such gigantic structures are symbols of prestige and power. They are monuments to the men or organizations that built them.

In some newly independent nations today governments have spent tremendous sums constructing huge official buildings. Critics of these buildings believe that the money could be put to better use building much needed schools and roads. But monument building, under different names, is an ancient preoccupation of the human race.

There is no reason to believe that the businessmen who ordered the construction of the World Trade Center, or the president of a newly independent nation who builds a huge presidential palace, think much differently from the pharaoh who ordered the building of a pyramid, the builders of Stonehenge in England, or the men who carved and erected the great statues of Easter Island. They all possessed the desire to build something large enough to impress their fellow man and to leave some sort of record of themselves for the future.

Today the job of building huge structures is a relatively easy one. With power machinery, moving a thousand-ton weight presents no particular problem. With our use of steel, and knowledge of building materials, we can routinely construct buildings hundreds of feet high. But for the man of ancient times, who possessed neither modern tools nor modern knowledge, the problem was considerably more difficult. There were also a lot fewer people in the world in ancient times. A big project involved the work of a larger percentage of the population, and a larger percentage of the people's total wealth.

The amount of work involved in building a monument such as the Great Pyramid of Egypt cannot really properly be compared with building a single skyscraper today. A better comparison might be with the work involved in building the entire United States network of superhighways. Work on superhighways was begun shortly after the end of World War II: Today, a quarter of a century later, it is not yet completed. The final cost will be hundreds of billions of dollars and the project will have used the labor of millions of men. The Great Pyramid must have involved a similar percentage of the national wealth and manpower of ancient Egypt.

Even with the simple methods at his command, ancient man solved the problems of moving great weights or raising tall monuments remarkably well. Within fairly recent times people who were not advanced, like the people of Easter Island, were still moving great weights with the methods that had first been used thousands of years ago and their stone-cutters were still using the same sort of simple tools.

The accomplishments of these ancient builders seemed miraculous. The monuments themselves are often surrounded by a reputation of mystery, romance and even terror.

At one time many believed that ancient peoples possessed secrets, either scientific or magical, which enabled them to move great stones with ease. Others looked at massive stone monuments and declared that they could only have been built by giants. Still others believed that the stones were alive and moved themselves. In Mexico stones that have been abandoned between the place they were cut and the monument for which they were intended are often called *piedras cansadas* or "tired stones."

There were no magical or other "lost secrets" needed to build the ancient monuments. While we often do not know the exact techniques and tools involved we do know, in a general way, how they were built. What was mostly involved was the lavish expenditure of two things—human time and human muscle power. Far more important than any engineering techniques was the ability of ancient societies to organize and direct the efforts of enormous numbers of people toward a single goal.

With the aid of modern machinery, a skyscraper can be put up in a few years with a crew of a few hundred men. But in ancient times thousands might have worked on a project that could have taken a century or more. These laborers had to be fed, clothed and housed, and all this took a great deal of wealth.

A band of hunters or a little village of simple farmers could never build a great monument, no matter how much they would have liked to. Even if they had the technical skills, they simply did not have enough manpower. Besides that, they had to spend a great deal of time just finding enough to eat. They never had a large enough food surplus to feed those who would have had to abandon the work of hunting or growing crops and spend all their time building.

Most monument-building societies also had a strong central leader, either a king or a tightly-knit ruling group. Without a strong direction the work of thousands could never have been organized.

Finally, the monument had to mean a great deal to those who built it in order to justify the time and effort. Not only did the monument have to have meaning to the leaders, it also had to be important to the common people—to those who did the hard physical labor needed. Most of those who did the work were not slaves. If slaves had been used the problems of organizing the job would have been much more difficult. Slaves hate their masters and do not work efficiently. Thousands of slaves massed together present a constant danger of revolt. An army of soldiers would have been needed to keep the army of slaves at work. These soldiers too would have to be fed, housed and clothed. The high cost of the building would get even higher. The men who did the backbreaking toil must have shared, at least to some extent, the aims of the leaders who ordered the construction.

In the chapters that follow, we will look at some ancient monuments from different parts of the world and from different periods of history. We will discuss who built them, how and why.

How do we know what methods were used? Ancient peoples did not write books on engineering. In many cases monuments were built by people who did not have any written language at all. Scientists must build up a case from clues, like a detective does.

Documents do provide some clues. Travelers or conquerors asked people how they built their monuments, and wrote down the answers they were given. Pictures may contain a hint of the methods used. An ancient Egyptian drawing of men moving a giant statue has given modern scientists a pretty good idea of how the Egyptians moved the huge blocks for their pyramids.

In other cases, unfinished work provides clues. Partially-cut stones in a quarry give scientists an idea of where the material for a particular monument came from and how the stone-cutting was done. In South America walls started but never finished by the Incas have ramps of earth built alongside. These ramps were clearly used to drag stones up to a higher part of the wall while it was being built. If the wall had been completed the ramp would have been taken down and we could never be sure it was used at all.

Sometimes we can experimentally recreate the conditions under which monuments were built. If modern men, using only ancient tools, can raise a particular stone or move it across the ground then we assume that ancient men could have done the same thing, and probably done it more efficiently because they had more practice.

Often scientists use what are called analogies. They reason that if one ancient society built a monument in a particular way then another one which had the same sort of tools probably used the same methods.

It is much harder to discover why a monument was built than how. But we must make an attempt to understand what drove people to engage in exhausting toil year in and year out. The real mystery of the ancient monuments is locked in the minds of those who planned them, and those who made the bricks and dragged the stones.

II
THE TOWER OF BABEL

PRACTICALLY EVERYONE HAS HEARD the story of the Tower of Babel. It is told in the first book of the Old Testament.

Some generations after the Flood of Noah's time all the people lived on a "plain in the land of Shi-nar." They all spoke one language. "And they said one to another, Go to, let us make bricks and burn them thoroughly. And they had brick for stone, and slime they had for mortar.

"And they said, Go to, let us build us a city and a tower, whose top may reach unto heaven; and let us make us a name, lest we be scattered abroad upon the face of the whole earth."

Here is one of the earliest written statements about an ancient monument. In it we find men expressing the desire to "make us a name," to gain some immortality and fame by building something very large.

The Lord looked down upon this show of human arrogance, and was displeased. He said, "Behold, the people is one, and they have all one language; and this they begin to do: and now nothing will be restrained from them which they have imagined to do."

So the Lord made the people speak many different languages, "That they may not understand one another's speech." And then he scattered them throughout the world. The construction of the great city and tower were abandoned.

"Therefore is the name of it called Babel; because the Lord did there confound the language of all the earth: and from thence did the Lord scatter them abroad upon the face of all the earth."

The word for this place of confusion is a part of our language today. We now spell it babble. When we cannot understand what a person is talking about, we often say he is babbling.

But there was a real ancient city called Babel, or Babylon. During the time in which the Old Testament was written, Babylon was one of the great cities of the world.

The story of the confusion of tongues at the Tower of Babel, may have started with an ancient pun. A pun is a joke where a word with one meaning is substituted for another which sounds the same, but has an entirely different meaning. There is a Hebrew word *balal*—which means to confuse. This sounds very much like Babel, an abbreviation for Babylon. Naturally, the name of the ancient city did not mean "confuse" in the language of those who lived there. In their language Babylon meant "the Gates of Heaven." But the similarity between the words would not have escaped the Hebrews who were bitter enemies of the people of Babylon.

The story of the Tower of Babel was probably written down about eight or nine hundred years before the beginning of the Christian era. It was no mere fable. At that time there was a real tower in Babylon which could have served as an inspiration for the tale. In fact, there are a number of towers on which the Bible story might have been based.

Babylon was located in a part of the world called Mesopotamia, the land between the two rivers. The rivers were the Tigris and Euphrates. Mesopotamia has been the home of many ancient civilizations. A regular feature of many Mesopotamian cities was great towers called ziggurats. Archaeologists have located the remains of some thirty of these structures.

Today even the best preserved of the towers is hardly more

than a pile of bricks. We can only guess what they looked like when they were in use. Fortunately, we have a description of a ziggurat in Babylon written by someone who claimed to have seen it.

That someone was Herodotus, a Greek writer who lived in the fifth century B.C. While still a young man Herodotus was exiled from his native city because he had become unpopular with the government. Being wealthy, and possessing an inexhaustible curiosity, Herodotus spent his time traveling around much of the known world. He looked and listened, and took notes on what he saw and heard. Later he wrote a sort of history of the world. Herodotus' books are the first of their kind ever written, and they have earned him the title of "father of history."

Herodotus said the ziggurat (although he did not call it that) was a temple dedicated to Bel, the chief god of Babylon. He said the temple was a square structure with great bronze gates. "It has a solid central tower . . . with a second erected on top of it and then a third, and so on up to eight. All eight towers can be climbed by a spiralway running round the outside, and about half way up there are seats for those who make the ascent to rest on. On the summit of the topmost tower stands a great temple with a fine large couch in it, richly covered, and a golden table."

Herodotus said that according to the Babylonians the god Bel would come down from the sky to sleep in the tower. But the Greek was careful to point out that he did not believe that story.

There is some doubt that Herodotus actually saw the ziggurat that stood in Babylon itself. From all other indications this structure was destroyed by one of the city's many conquerors before Herodotus was born, and it was never rebuilt. However, the memory of such an imposing tower must have been strong. People would undoubtedly have been able to tell Herodotus what it had looked like.   It is also probable that Herodotus saw some of Mesopotamia's other ziggurats.   Archaeologists who have attempted to reconstruct a picture of what the original ziggurat of Babylon looked like believe that Herodotus' description was accurate.

We cannot tell when the first ziggurat was built in Babylon. But the tower was undoubtedly destroyed and rebuilt many times.   The final rebuilding came around 600 B.C. during the reign of King Nebuchadnezzar II.   This ziggurat may have reached a height of 300 feet.   Like all ziggurats it was basically a series of blocks piled upon one another.   The largest block was at the bottom, the smallest at the top.   The exterior of the ziggurat was covered with brightly colored enameled bricks. In the blazing sunlight of Mesopotamia, the ziggurat of Babylon would have been an awe-inspiring sight.   It was striking enough to be remembered by men for centuries after it had disappeared from the face of the earth.

While the ziggurat of Babylon is entirely gone, the ruins of some of the other ziggurats of Mesopotamia remain.   Perhaps the best preserved of these are the ruins of the tower of the city of Ur.

Ur is one of the oldest cities in the world.   It was deserted thousands of years ago when the Euphrates river changed course. The sands drifted over its ruins, and everybody forgot where it had been located.

The sand-covered remains of Ur looked like hills.   Even the towering pile which covered the remains of the great ziggurat looked like a natural part of the landscape.   But those few travelers who passed the desolate spot where the great city had once flourished noted that just under the sand they could find bricks. When archaeologists uncovered the remains of Ur, they found that the first people to live in the city were the Sumerians, the oldest civilization in Mesopotamia, and perhaps the first civilization in the entire world.

All the ziggurats—indeed almost all the structures of Mesopotamian civilization—were built of brick. Mesopotamia is a land that contains few trees and very little natural rock. The only practical building material in such a land is clay and mud.

Mesopotamian builders used two kinds of brick in their construction. The simplest was sun-dried mud brick. Mud was put into a rectangular mold and left out to dry in the sun. The mud would dry into a rock-hard brick. Mud brick is easy to make, but it has one major drawback: if mud brick gets too wet it turns back into mud. It doesn't rain very often in Mesopotamia so mud brick is perfectly adequate for building simple dwellings. It is still used for building in many dry parts of the world today. If a hut is destroyed during one of the infrequent rainstorms, it can be quickly and cheaply rebuilt. But for larger and more permanent structures like the ziggurat a more durable material had to be used.

At some point early in the history of Mesopotamian civilization the builders discovered that bricks which had been heated to a very high temperature in a furnace were much stronger and more resistant to moisture than those which had simply been dried in the sun. These fired, or burnt, bricks were more difficult and expensive to produce. They would have been particularly hard to make in Mesopotamia where there was very little wood available to heat the furnaces to fire the bricks.

The builders tried to be as frugal as they could. The core of the ziggurat tower was made of mud brick. This was encased in an outside layer of stronger burnt brick, many feet thick.

Water from rains or floods might still be absorbed from the ground by the mud brick. This would cause the bricks to

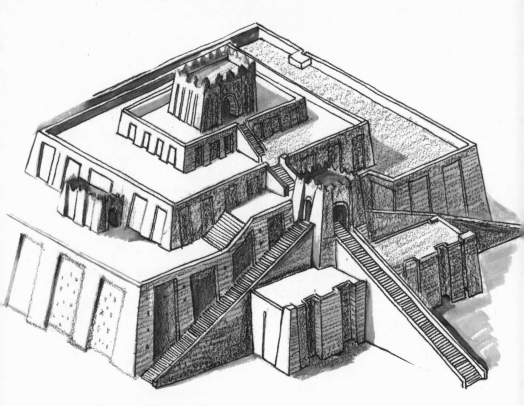

Reconstruction of the ziggurat at Ur.

swell. If the builders had not taken precautions the swelling
mud bricks would have burst the casing of burnt brick. But
ziggurats contained many drainage ducts, called "weeper holes."
These were cut through the burnt brick and allowed the excess
moisture from the interior bricks to drain off harmlessly.

Substances such as pitch and bitumen were used as mortar.
Not only did these substances help to hold the bricks together,
they also helped protect them from moisture. Pitch and bitumen are natural products of oil. They are found in abundance
in many parts of the oil-rich Middle East.

The ziggurat is not a very complicated structure. The tower
was a solid pile of bricks. It contained no rooms or chambers.
Its sole purpose was to put the temple at an imposing height.
Mesopotamia is one of the flattest places in the world, and this
artificial mountain could not help but be impressive. A temple

atop such a monument would certainly seem a fit dwelling place for the chief god. The people of Mesopotamia were very religious. It is not surprising that they should spend a great deal of time and energy building such a monument.

The building of a ziggurat was a huge undertaking. The builders had to have the technical skills needed for making bricks and laying them properly. Even more important, they had to live in the sort of society where the labor of large numbers of people could be organized and directed toward a single end.

The origin of the civilization of Mesopotamia is mysterious. By this we mean we do not know where it began because we do not have enough facts available. As far as archaeologists have yet been able to determine, civilization appeared in the land between the two rivers almost full grown. The basic features of these societies were already established when they entered the archaeological record. These features remained essentially unchanged for thousands of years.

We know that civilizations do not just spring up full grown. Many scientists believe that Mesopotamian civilization developed slowly right in Mesopotamia, but that the archaeologists have not found all the evidence yet. Others think that civilized people first came to Mesopotamia as immigrants.

If this theory is correct, then we must look for the origins of civilization elsewhere. But where? The ziggurats may provide a clue. According to one theory, civilization began in a mountainous or hilly region—perhaps the Iranian highlands to the north, or somewhere in the mountains of Asia to the east of Mesopotamia. The people of these regions may have worshipped their gods on mountain tops, or believed that their gods lived on the tops of mountains. Many ancient peoples who lived in mountainous regions held such beliefs.

When these mountain people came to the flat Tigris and

Euphrates valley they built the ziggurats as artificial mountains, in memory of their original homeland.

But as we said, this is all theory. At our present state of knowledge, we cannot determine if the earliest civilized people of Mesopotamia came from somewhere else, or were influenced by peoples of another region. We do know that the Mesopotamians influenced many other ancient peoples. Perhaps their most important influence was on the developing civilization of Egypt in the valley of the Nile River.

III
THE PYRAMIDS

ABOUT A CENTURY and a half before the birth of Christ a Greek mathematician, Philon of Byzantium, wrote a little book called *The Seven Wonders of the World*. In the book he gave a brief description of the seven most remarkable monuments that he had ever heard of.

The monuments were tombs, temples, statues and other structures of unusual size. By the time Philon wrote, most of these wonders had already been destroyed. Today only one of Philon's seven wonders of the world remains. It is the Great Pyramid of Egypt.

The Great Pyramid is the largest of Egypt's many pyramids. It has endured because it is so huge and so solidly built, that before the invention of high explosives it was impossible to destroy.

The Great Pyramid is not only the sole surviving "wonder of the world," it was the oldest structure on Philon's list. For many centuries before Philon wrote, travelers had been coming to Egypt to stare in amazement at the Great Pyramid and the other Egyptian pyramids. One of these travelers was Herodotus, the man who had visited the ziggurats of Mesopotamia.

It was natural that Herodotus should visit Egypt. The Greeks believed Egypt to be the oldest of all lands and a storehouse of the world's wisdom. No one as inquisitive as Herodotus could possibly overlook the ancient kingdom on the Nile.

Like most modern tourists in Egypt, Herodotus had to see the pyramids. Herodotus lived nearly 2,500 years ago. He is part ancient history to us. Yet to him the pyramids were ancient history. They were nearly as ancient to Herodotus as Herodotus is to us.

Egyptian guides took Herodotus to Giza, a flat region just a few miles outside of what is now Cairo, the capital of Egypt. At Giza are Egypt's three greatest pyramids. The guides told the Greek traveler that the largest of the three pyramids had been built by a king called Cheops. This king, the guides asserted, was a brutal tyrant and the huge pyramid was a monument to his tyranny.

According to the guides, "Cheops brought the country into all sorts of misery. He closed all the temples, then, not content with excluding his subjects from the practice of their religion, compelled them without exception to labor as slaves for his own advantage."

Herodotus' Egyptian guides told him a lot of other things about the pyramids. Some of these things were true, but many were not. Like guides of all ages, they liked to tell the tourists a good story to earn a few extra coins. It didn't matter whether the story was the truth. The guides probably did not know what was the truth. The pyramids, after all, were ancient history to them too.

One thing Herodotus' guides told him that certainly was true was that the pyramids were tombs for the pharaohs or god kings of Egypt. But they were not just monuments to the insane vanity of the kings. To understand why the pyramids were built we have to know something about the ancient Egyptian attitude toward their kings and toward death.

Egyptian civilization began to develop some six thousand years ago. At first the people lived in a number of little kingdoms scattered along the banks of the Nile. By 3,000 B.C. all

these kingdoms had been consolidated under the rule of a single great king or pharaoh. To the Egyptians their king was much more than a leader. He was a living god. The people not only served him, they worshipped him.

The Egyptians had a complicated set of beliefs about death. When a man died his body was carefully preserved and buried in the largest tomb he could afford. For this reason a lot of people today think that the ancient Egyptians were a morbid people, obsessed with death. This is not true. The Egyptians were cheerful and they loved life. They expected the good life on this earth to continue in some form after death. Being a practical people they assumed that the objects they had enjoyed in this world would be needed in the next. So they were buried with all their personal possessions.

An Egyptian believed that if his spirit were to be happy in the next world, his body had to be preserved. The preserved body or mummy was to be a resting place for the spirit. Therefore, the Egyptians spent a lot of time and money building tombs for their mummies and the treasures buried with them.

There was another compelling reason for a large tomb. Egyptian religion stressed that a dead man should not be forgotten. So long as a man's name was remembered, said the Egyptians, he would continue to live in the next world. The larger his tomb the more likely it was that the dead man would be remembered.

What better way was there for the pharaoh, the most powerful and richest man in all Egypt, to fulfill all these needs than to build a tomb of overpowering size and magnificence?

The earliest pharaohs had been buried in underground chambers. Above the chambers a solid box-like structure called a mastaba was built. The early mastabas were usually made of brick.

Around the year 2,700 B.C. a king called Zoser was buried under a very different sort of structure—this was the first pyramid. Zoser's pyramid did not look like the smooth triangular pyramid that most of us have seen in pictures. It looks like six huge blocks piled atop one another. The higher the block, the smaller. The result was what we call today the Step Pyramid. It is located at Sakkara, not far from Cairo, or from the more famous pyramids at Giza.

The design and construction of the Step Pyramid is attributed to a man called Imhotep, a member of Zoser's court. In later ages the Egyptians worshipped Imhotep as a god. They said he had invented all manner of wonderful things. Today some experts consider him to be the world's first scientist and engineer.

Modern scientists who have studied the Step Pyramid believe that the idea for this unusual structure grew slowly by trial and error. First Imhotep had a single large mastaba constructed. Then probably in order to make the king's tomb look larger and more impressive he had two smaller mastabas built on top of the first. At this point he conceived an even bolder plan. He had the original three "steps" enlarged, and three more built on top of them. The result was the six-tiered Step Pyramid.

The Step Pyramid was constructed of blocks of cut stone. It is the first large stone structure in the world. Since stone is much more durable than brick, the Step Pyramid still stands today.

The design was a great success and later pharaohs tried to imitate Zoser's tomb, and to improve upon it. But attempts at improving the design did not always work.

At a spot called Meidum in the desert, there is another Step Pyramid. This one is surrounded by a huge mound of rubble. Archaeologists believe that the builders at Meidum had tried to build the first smooth-sided or "true" pyramid. They started with a Step Pyramid and then filled in the steps with blocks of stone. But the design was not stable. Sometime, perhaps while the pyramid was still being built, the outside material slipped off in a catastrophic accident. All that is left standing are the original steps. The pyramid may never have been finished, and we are not sure which king it was meant for.

At a place called Dashur there is another example of pyramid construction that did not work as originally planned. This structure is called the Bent Pyramid. The original plan called for the pyramid to rise at a fairly steep angle. But about one-third of the way up the angle was changed to a much shallower one. What caused the change of plan? Some believe the pharaoh died while the pyramid was being built and the builders simply decided to finish up the job quickly. Perhaps the Bent Pyramid was under construction when the pyramid at Meidum collapsed. The builders would then have realized that such a steep pyramid was unstable. To avoid a similar accident they altered the angle. If the stones were not piled so steeply, they reasoned, then they would not slide off the pyramid.

The Bent Pyramid was built for King Snefru who died in 2,592 B.C. Snefru also had a second pyramid built for himself at Dashur. This pyramid was not bent, nor did it collapse. By that time the Egyptian engineers had mastered the art of building a true pyramid.

The stage was not set for the construction of the largest and most famous of all pyramids—the Great Pyramid at Giza. The king for whom this tomb was built was Khufu (Greeks like Herodotus called him Cheops). He was Snefru's successor, probably his son, and he ruled Egypt from about 2,592 B.C. to 2,569 B.C.

Khufu's pyramid is truly a man-made mountain. It stands nearly 500 feet high and is over 750 feet on each side at the base. It covers an area of some 571,000 square feet, or about thirteen acres. It is the largest tomb ever built, and one of the largest structures of any kind to be built until the introduction of modern machinery.

Although it is nearly 5,000 years old the Great Pyramid is still very impressive. But it is nowhere near as impressive today as it was when it was first built. Now the outside of the pyramid looks as though it was made of brownish blocks. Originally these blocks were covered by a layer of white polished limestone. The limestone made the surface absolutely smooth and gleaming from top to bottom. Through the centuries this limestone has been stripped away and used for buildings in Cairo.

The Great Pyramid today is also surrounded by a lot of rubble. This is all that remains of a virtual city of temples, and smaller tombs for the wives and officials of the pharaoh.

At Giza there are two other pyramids, built by two of Khufu's successors. The pyramid of the pharaoh Khephren is slightly smaller than the Great Pyramid of Khufu. Khephren's pyramid looks larger at a distance because it is built on higher ground. The third pyramid, that of Mykerinus, is considerably smaller than the other two.

Zoser's Step Pyramid was solid. It was built on top of a network of underground chambers and tunnels. The king himself was buried inside of one of these chambers. Most of the other Egyptian pyramids are also either solid, or contain very tiny interior rooms. In most cases the pharaohs were buried, like Zoser, under the pyramid. The pyramids were not really buildings, but rather huge tombstones or markers.

The Great Pyramid of Khufu is different. It does contain interior chambers, although they are still quite small. Archaeologists believe that the king's mummy was placed inside of one of these chambers. We do not know for sure since all of the pyramids were thoroughly emptied out by tomb robbers thousands of years ago. Not one of the mummies of the pyramid-building pharaohs has ever been found. In that sense the pyramids were failures, for they did not protect either the bodies or the treasures of the kings.

The Great Pyramid contains two interior chambers and one underground chamber. The larger of the inside chambers presumably held the king's mummy. Whether the other two chambers had some purpose, a storehouse for treasure or perhaps dummy chambers to mislead tomb robbers, we do not know. It is most probable that they are merely the result of a change of plan in the construction, and were not used at all.

The main interior chamber of the Great Pyramid was broken into in ancient times and later sealed up again, perhaps several times. Herodotus knew about the passage to the main inside chamber 2,500 years ago. But the Caliph Al Mamun who

Cross-section of the Great Pyramid.

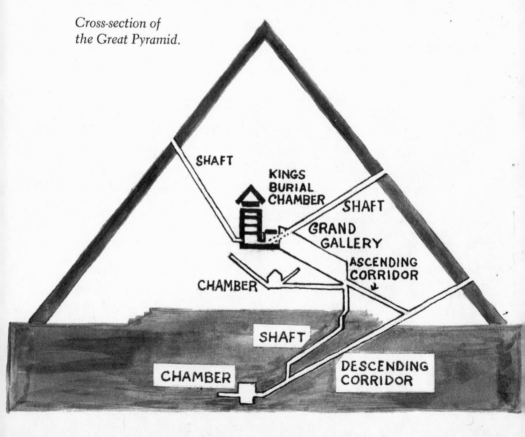

ruled Egypt a little over a thousand years ago did not. He suspected that there was a treasure buried somewhere inside the pyramid, and he was determined to get at it. He had his men chop a tunnel right through the pyramid. When they had dug for about 200 feet they heard a crash to their left. They began working in that direction and discovered an interior passage that led to the main chamber. The noise had been caused by a slab of rock that had fallen out of the roof of the passage.

The account of what the Caliph's men found inside the Great Pyramid is not clear. All that is left there now is a lidless black granite sarcophagus. We do not even know if it ever contained the mummy of the king, because it looks as though it was never finished. The sarcophagus is too large to have been dragged up the entire passage. It must have been put in place during construction, and then the rest of the pryamid was built around it.

The Great Pyramid was constructed for the dead not for the living, and the living entered it at their peril. In 1579 a man named Johannes Helffrich wrote in his journal of a visit inside the Great Pyramid.

"We climbed a high corridor which lay straight before us, with great difficulty, because this corridor was both wide and extremely high. On the sides of the wall, set back at about half a man's height, are holes each a good pace distant from the next; we had to hold onto these and climb up as best we could."

In the main chamber the atmosphere was so foul, and the visitors became "so full of this same unhealthy air that the following night we fell into such weariness and weakness that within two days, we could stir neither arm nor leg." Today it is not so dangerous to enter the Great Pyramid, but the guidebooks still warn of the very hot and musty atmosphere.

Many have speculated that other pyramids might also contain

hidden and undiscovered rooms. Today we cannot simply chop through the pyramids like Caliph Al Mamun's workmen did. In the late 1960s scientists using a technique very much like that used in X-rays tried to determine if there were any hidden chambers in other pyramids. They found nothing, but the results are still not entirely conclusive. Pyramids might yet contain some tiny, unknown chambers.

Visitors to the pyramids are amazed that they were built at all. The ancient Egyptians had only the simplest of tools. They had no horses or other work animals to drag the huge blocks that make up the pyramids. All these had to be dragged by gangs of men.

The Egyptians did not use horses because there were none in Egypt in those early days. There were other animals that might have been used to drag stones, but the Egyptians did not have the equipment to harness them properly. The only kind of harness the early Egyptians had was a loop that fitted over an animal's neck. If an animal was forced to drag a heavy load this sort of harness would choke it. Under such conditions a man was a much more efficient beast of burden.

Some of the stones for the pyramids were quarried far up the Nile and floated to Giza on barges. They were then dragged up from the river to the building site itself. The Egyptians did not put the blocks on wheeled carts. They knew how to use the wheel, but it would have been difficult to construct carts strong enough to hold the massive blocks. Rollers—logs or other cylindrical objects—might have been placed under the blocks to make pulling easier. As the block was pulled forward the roller from the back would be carried up front. The result would be a continuous roadway of rollers.

But we do not know that the Egyptians used rollers. The blocks might have been mounted on sledges, platforms with runners. The runners would then be greased by pouring water or milk under them to make them slide more easily. One Egyptian drawing shows a huge statue being pulled by a gang of men. The statue is tied to a platform with runners. One man is pouring some sort of liquid in front of the runners.

Once the blocks were at the base of the pyramid how were they put into place on the upper tiers? Most of the experts on ancient Egypt believe that the pyramid builders used a huge ramp of mud and rubble to drag the blocks to the upper tiers. This ramp might have been built up alongside one face of the pyramid. As the pyramid grew higher the ramp could be made both higher and longer, so that the angle at which the blocks had to be dragged would not increase. Another possibility is that a spiral ramp was built up around all sides of the pyramid.

The average block in the Great Pyramid weighs about two and one half tons. Eight or ten men could drag such a block along the level ground. At least twice that number would be needed to pull it up a ramp. Some of the stones on the inside of the pyramid or at the very top were considerably larger than two and one half tons.

We know that the Egyptians did use ramps in building some pyramids. The remains of these ramps have been found alongside of unfinished pyramids. But engineers have never been entirely comfortable with the ramp theory for the Great Pyramid. They insist that building a ramp big enough to accommodate the 480 foot structure would have been a harder job than building the pyramid itself. Some doubt that there was enough manpower in ancient Egypt to build such a ramp. Engineers also doubt that there would have been enough room at the top of the ramp to accommodate the number of men needed to pull up the huge top stone for the pyramid.

Herodotus' guides told him that the ancient builders used

some sort of wooden crane or hoist that lifted the blocks from tier to tier. Unfortunately Herodotus' description of this device was not very clear. Most scholars believe that the guides simply did not know what they were talking about.

But Olaf Tellefsen, an engineer who has long been interested in how ancient structures were built, believes he has identified this mysterious wooden lifting device. He believes it is a weight arm, a form of lever that has been used by many ancient peoples, but is almost forgotten today.

Tellefsen once watched modern Egyptians using a weight arm to move two ton blocks. With the device three men were able to lift the blocks. Says Tellefsen, "The primitive piece of equipment the men were using was a triumph of elementary physics—a large weight arm, consisting of a heavy timber that pivoted on a sturdy, 6-foot-high fulcrum. The short arm was less than 3 feet long; the long arm 15 to 16 feet. A pallet was attached to the long arm, upon which rocks could be piled for counterweight."

One of the Egyptians put a sling under a large stone, and attached it to the short end of the weight arm. The other two piled rocks on the pallet until it almost balanced, then by pulling on the weight arm they brought the beam down and lifted the stone about a foot off the ground. The stone was then easily lowered onto planks, rollers and a pair of runners.

Said Tellefsen, "I felt sure the apparatus I had seen must have been based on an idea inherited from the past, where it had played a key role in raising of huge stone structures of the past, including the Great Pyramid."

With the aid of the weight arm Tellefsen thinks that the ancient Egyptians could have made much better use of skids and rollers than previously believed. It is easy to lift large blocks onto them with a weight arm. He thinks that the

Egyptians might have built wooden tracks and laid them directly up the side of the pyramid. The blocks would then be lifted, by means of a weight arm, onto a heavily greased sledge. A gang of twenty or thirty men at the top of the pyramid could then have pulled the block up the wooden track. Another weight arm would be used to lift the block off the sledge. It could then be dragged on rollers and pushed into place.

Various combinations of weight arms, or simple modifications, could have been used to move the really huge stones and slabs for the interior passages and chambers, Tellefsen thinks.

The amount of time and labor needed to build the Great Pyramid was staggering. Herodotus' guides told him that 100,000 slaves labored for over twenty years on it. As usual the guides seem to have been exaggerating. While digging in the area around the Great Pyramid, archaeologists have found the remains of housing for about 4,000 men. Scientists believe that this housing was for men who worked on the pyramid. But 4,000 men would have been only the permanent staff—those who worked year-round. Among them would have been engineers, stonemasons and other skilled workmen. At certain times of the year many ordinary laborers, the men who dragged the stones, would have been engaged in the project. Perhaps at these times the work force neared 100,000.

But the laborers were not slaves; they were probably unemployed farmers. During one season of the year, the Nile River overflows its banks and floods the fields of Egypt. The annual Nile flood is necessary for Egyptian agriculture. Rain is infrequent in Egypt and most water comes from the Nile. But while the fields were flooded or muddy no farming could be carried on. The season of the flood would also be the best season for floating the blocks for the pyramid from where they were quarried.

This brings up another possible reason why the pyramids were built. Some scholars think that they were built in part just to give people something to do while they could not work their fields. It is always dangerous for a state to have large numbers of unemployed people. During the time the pyramids were being built, Egypt had not been a unified land that long. People who had nothing else to do might fall to fighting with one another as they had in the old days. This sort of turmoil would threaten the power of the pharaoh. So he may have wanted to keep his subjects occupied until they could get back to tilling their fields. For their part, the people may have been happy, even for the backbreaking work of dragging huge stones. They were undoubtedly fed and clothed at the pharaoh's expense. If they did not have this source of food the season of the flood could have been a time of extreme hardship for the poor.

The people might also have felt honored to work on the pharaoh's tomb. He was, after all, the chief god of Egypt. To work for his greater glory would have been a religious obligation.

All this, of course, is guesswork. We really have no idea what went through the mind of the pharaoh, or of the ordinary man who dragged the heavy stone blocks for his tomb. But this much we can be sure of—those who labored on the pyramids were not merely slaves driven by a tyrant's whip.

Herodotus' guides told him that the Egyptians so hated Khufu and his pyramid-building successor Khephren, that they could hardly bring themselves to mention those names. But archaeologists have unearthed many documents with stories from ancient Egypt in which Khufu is pictured as a wise and kindly ruler.

There also seems to be no truth to the belief that the building of the Great Pyramid was so expensive that it ruined the country. Egypt remained stable and prosperous long after Khufu's death.

Ancient Egyptian civilization lasted for about 4,000 years—much longer than any other civilization on earth. Yet the time of pyramid-building was remarkably brief. All of the large pyramids of Egypt were built in the century that followed the construction of the Step Pyramid, the first to be built. This raises two questions: why did the Egyptians use the pyramid shape for tombs in the first place? and why did they stop using it?

A lot of different answers have been proposed for the first question. Many believe that the pyramid shape had some sort of sacred significance for the Egyptians. But there is no proof of this. A physicist named Kurt Mendelssohn who has been interested in the pyramids has given a surprisingly simple answer to the question of why the pyramid shape was used: it was used because with the technical knowledge they possessed the Egyptians could build the largest possible structure in that shape. You can test this yourself on the beach. Try to build the highest possible mound of sand. What shape will it be? It will be in the shape of a pyramid, or a cone, which is very nearly the same thing. A structure with a broad base and a narrow top is the most stable. For a people who are technologically not very advanced it is the easiest thing to build. The ziggurats of Mesopotamia were very like the Step Pyramid.

Writes Mendelssohn: "Five thousand years ago, for the first time in history, man had changed the skyline of the world by building mountains with his own hands. There must have been tremendous pride of achievement and this we may perhaps find the cost compelling reason for erecting the pyramids. They were built because man had reached the stage at which he was able to build them."

Why did pyramid-building come to an end? Perhaps, after a century, the Egyptians realized that pyramids, though impressive in size, were just not doing the job of protecting the pharaoh's mummy. Perhaps the techniques of building smaller, but better tombs for their rulers had been perfected by the Egyptians. And possibly the pharaoh no longer felt that it was necessary to launch a huge public works project to keep his subjects busy.

Whatever the reason or reasons, intensive pyramid-building stopped. A few smaller pyramids continued to be built over the next few thousand years. But these in no way compare with the pyramids at Giza, Dashur, Sakkara and Meidum. But during that brief period the ancient Egyptians produced some of the most impressive and durable monuments ever created by man.

IV
STONEHENGE

STONEHENGE IS THE MOST CELEBRATED ancient monument in the British Isles. It seemed a mysterious place, and to writers of fiction it became a haunted place, a place of terror and danger. In one story the hero comes across an old book in which he reads:

" 'ELEMENTALS OF STONEHENGE. Though the day of the Druids is now long passed and the cries of their victims no longer haunt the night and the altar stone has ceased to drip blood, yet it is dangerous to go there when the sacrificial moon is full. For the Druids, by the blood they shed, their vile sacrifices and fellowship with the devil, attracted forces of evil to the place. So it is said that shapeless invisible horrors haunt the vicinity and at certain times crave a resting place in a human body. If one they enter in, it is only with difficulty that they are evicted.' "

But Stonehenge is not haunted and did not inspire terror in every heart, though people have puzzled over it for centuries. Today such monuments are called megalithic which means that they were built from large stones, or megaliths. Stonehenge is not the only megalithic in the world, but it is the most famous.

Stonehenge never had to be discovered. As far as the people of the British Isles were concerned, it had always been there. It is located right in the middle of the pleasant agricultural region called Salisbury Plain. Stonehenge had been built so long ago that no one remembered who built it or how or why. In fact

they could not even remember why it was called Stonehenge.

The name Stonehenge did not appear in writing until the twelfth century. A historian named Henry of Huntington first called the old monument Stonehenge. He said the name meant "hanging stones" because the stones, "hang as it were in the air."

The most striking feature of Stonehenge are arrangements that look like gateways. These consist of three huge stones— two elongated uprights or pillars set near one another, and a third stone called a lintel perched on top of the uprights. To some it may have seemed as if the lintel stone quite literally hung in the air.

A more colorful explanation for the name was that condemned criminals were hung from the stones. But this probably never happened.

During the Middle Ages many people simply could not believe that ordinary men had been able to move such enormous stones. Some said that Stonehenge had been built in ancient times by giants who had once inhabited the earth. Others believed that the stones had been moved by magic. There were legends which told how the great magician Merlin had brought the stones from Ireland at the request of King Arthur's father. They were set up in England as a memorial to warriors slain in a battle.

But the more people of Britain began to learn about their own past the more they doubted that Stonehenge had been built by giants or by Merlin's magic. Over the centuries the British Isles had been conquered by many different peoples. Stonehenge was attributed to one or the other of these conquerors. A popular candidate was the Romans, who had ruled Britain in the first four centuries of the Christian era.

The Romans certainly had the technical know-how to build

such a monument. But Stonehenge does not look like anything ever built by the Romans. As it turned out, Stonehenge was standing long before the Romans arrived. The Romans themselves doubtless puzzled over the huge stones just as later peoples did.

Most popular candidates for the builders of Stonehenge were the Druids. The Druids were a rather mysterious group. They were the priests and leaders of the Celtic peoples who had once ruled the British Isles. The Druids first came to Britain three or four hundred years B.C. They did practice human sacrifice, but so did a lot of other ancient peoples. They were still very powerful when the Romans conquered Britain in 43 A.D. The Druids helped to lead the resistance to the Romans. As a result the all-conquering Romans practically wiped them out, so we do not know too much about them. But we do know this much—the Druids did not build Stonehenge. It was there when they arrived.

We have to repeat that the Druids did not build Stonehenge because the belief that they did is still very popular today. There is a cult which claims to be the direct descendants of the ancient Druids. On June 22, the longest day of the year, these modern "Druids" put on white robes and troop out to Stonehenge to greet the rising sun. There are no sacrifices, just some harmless chanting. They say that this is part of an age-old ceremony that has been performed at Stonehenge for over three thousand years. Scholars disagree with this statement. They point out that there is no evidence that the Druids ever used Stonehenge as a place of worship. The Druids seemed to prefer groves of trees for their rites. Since no one knows what the ancient Druids really did, the scholars say that the modern "Druids" have made up their ceremony.

Well then, who did build Stonehenge? Archaeologists call

the builders of Stonehenge the Wessex people. The area in which the monument is located was once called Wessex. We have no idea what the builders called themselves and Wessex people is just a convenient label.

When the Wessex people began to build Stonehenge they were at a stage of culture called neolithic (that is, from the New Stone Age). This means that most of their tools were made from stone or bone. With these simple materials neolithic man fashioned tools that were surprisingly efficient.

The early Wessex people lived by farming and herding. Life was simple and hard—but it would be wrong to think that the Wessex people were some sort of not-quite-human "prehistoric men" or "cave men." They were completely modern in the biological sense of the word. When the Wessex people started to build Stonehenge, the civilizations of Mesopotamia and Egypt were already thousands of years old.

We cannot be sure when the building of Stonehenge began. The best guess is that it was started around 2,000 B.C. However, some recent studies indicate that construction may have started five to seven hundred years earlier than that. The construction was carried out in three stages over a period of several hundred years.

During the first stage of its construction Stonehenge may not have had any stones in it. The basic feature of this stage of Stonehenge—called Stonehenge I by the archaeologists—was two circular banks or walls of earth. These made a circle about 300 feet across. The outer bank was two or three feet high and six feet wide. The inner bank was six feet high and twenty feet wide. Separating them was a ditch from which the material to pile up the banks was dug.

These banks of earth have been much worn down over the centuries. Now they are covered with grass. But when they were first built they would have looked very different. The soil of Salisbury Plain is chalky, hard and white. The high banks would have been gleaming white walls against the grassy plane.

There is a gap in the northeast side of the circular walls. Through this runs the Avenue, an ancient roadway which connects Stonehenge with the River Avon, two miles away. The Avenue was also bounded by a bank and ditch.

The digging was carried out with picks made from the antlers of the red deer. Many broken antlers were found at the bottom of the ditch. Modern tests have shown antler picks to be almost as good as metal-headed picks for digging.

In the center of the Avenue, just outside of the circle, is the oldest and most famous of all the stones of Stonehenge—the Heel Stone. This rough-textured megalith which stands some fifteen feet high and may weigh over thirty-five tons is the only stone which could have been part of the construction of Stonehenge I. It is made from a type of natural sandstone called sarsen. The name comes from the word Saracen (Moslem). It was first applied to the boulders at Stonehenge because they do not come from Salisbury Plain (which has no natural rock) but like the Saracens, were thought to come from some place exotic and far away. In fact, all the sarsens were brought from Marlborough Downs, which is not very exotic, and only about twenty miles from Stonehenge.

How the Heel Stone got its name is unknown. Like most of the names of individual stones at Stonehenge—the Altar Stone, the Slaughter Stone, etc.—the name Heel Stone was probably tacked on to it quite late in its history.

Inside the inner bank is a circle of fifty-six holes. These are called the Aubrey Holes, in honor of John Aubrey, the man who discovered them.

That is just about all there was to Stonehenge I. The bank

and ditch could have been dug by a couple of hundred men in a single summer.

A century or two after Stonehenge I was completed, the Wessex people began an ambitious addition to their monument. This new burst of building enthusiasm seems to have coincided with the arrival of a new people in the vicinity of Salisbury Plain —the Beaker people. They got their name from a particular sort of pottery that they used. Traces of this pottery have been found in Spain up through France and all over the British Isles. Aside from their pottery these people brought with them the use of bronze tools. Did the Beaker people come as conquerors or peaceful migrants? We do not know for sure, but they shortly seemed to blend in with the native Wessex people.

During the building of Stonehenge II the bluestones were added. In many respects this was the most remarkable part of the building of Stonehenge. Despite their name these stones usually look grayish, not blue, but when they are wet they show a faint bluish tinge. There is only one place in the world that this particular type of stone could come from. That is the Prescelly Mountains in Wales, some 130 miles from Stonehenge. Originally there were about 80 bluestones in Stonehenge, and they weighed up to five tons each.

How could these stones have been brought from Wales to Salisbury Plain? The easiest way would have been to load them on rafts and float them through bays and rivers. In this way the stones would be floated about 215 miles over water. But they still would have to be dragged overland for about 25 miles.

In 1954 the British Broadcasting Corporation tried to recreate the moving of the bluestones for a special television program about Stonehenge. For the bluestones the B.B.C. used concrete slabs weighing up to four tons. Sturdy college students were enlisted to move the slabs using only the materials that

Moving the bluestones by water.

would have been originally available to the Wessex people.

Water transport turned out to be quite easy. Four men could guide a raft with a slab on it through shallow water. With practice the job probably could have been done by a single man. Moving the slab over the land was much more difficult. All methods were tried—the slabs were simply dragged, they were lashed to a sledge or they were put on rollers. Still it took sixteen men a day to move a one-ton slab a mile or less. The pyramid builders could move stones more efficiently —but they were moving them over level ground and in the desert where they had no underbrush to contend with.

Granted that the Wessex people were probably better at moving the bluestones than the college students were at moving the concrete slabs, the task was still enormous.

The next stage of Stonehenge (Stonehenge III) involved moving the great sandstone sarsens from Marlborough Downs.

The builders undoubtedly started by trying to find natural boulders of appropriate size and shape. Larger boulders had to be cut down to the proper size, and chunks of rock had to be quarried directly out of the side of the downs. The methods used were simple, crude and time-consuming. But they worked. They must have been the same as those used to quarry the bluestones in Wales.

Rocks could be cracked by building a fire on them. The fire would be built along a line where the quarryman wanted the rock to crack. It would then be doused with cold water. The sudden change in temperature could produce a crack. This crack could be enlarged by forcing a wooden wedge into it, then soaking the wedge with water so it would swell. The quarry men would also have looked for convenient natural cracks in the rock. The crude shaping was done by banging away at one rock with another. The Wessex people at this point possessed metal tools, but these were too soft and brittle to be of much use in stone-working.

Then came the problem of moving the sarsens, which averaged forty tons each. They must have been moved overland the same way the bluestones were, by being dragged on sledges or rollers. Some scientists have suggested that the stones were moved only during the winter months when they could be slid with greater ease over frozen ground.

Whatever the method or methods used, it would have taken a thousand men at least seven years to move all the sarsens to Salisbury Plain.

Once at the site of Stonehenge, the sarsens had to be dressed or finished. The Heel Stone is rough and pitted. It must have been set up in the condition in which it was found. But the other sarsens and the bluestones are all smooth and shaped. Stones may have been smoothed by dragging one across another many, many times. Perhaps sand mixed with water was sprinkled between the stones to make the grinding more effective.

Today Stonehenge is a ruin, although an imposing one. Most of the sarsens and bluestones have either fallen over or have disappeared entirely. But archaeologists have a pretty good idea of what it looked like when it was first completed.

Inside the bank and ditch was the sarsen circle. This was a closed circle of thirty huge sarsen pillars, joined at the top by thirty slightly curvel lintels.

The largest of the sarsens were used to make the sarsen horseshoe, which stood inside the sarsen circle. The sarsen horseshoe originally consisted of five giant trilithons—sets of three stones. Each contained two uprights, weighing perhaps forty-five tons each, topped by a lintel. The total effect was to form a sort of doorway. A narrow one though, for the space between the uprights was only about twelve inches. The open end of the horseshoe faced toward the Avenue.

Between the two sarsen structures there was a circle of sixty bluestones. These may once have been capped by lintels to to form a miniature replica of the sarsen circle. Inside the sarsen horseshoe was a smaller horseshoe of bluestones. Scientists are not quite sure of the placement of the bluestones. They seem to have been moved a number of times during construction. Most of the bluestones have long since disappeared. They were broken up and carted away by farmers and souvenir hunters before Stonehenge became a protected national monument.

In addition to these main structures, there were other pillar-like stones in various spots around the circle. Aside from the Aubrey Holes, there are also several other circles of holes of varying sizes. Stonehenge may once have contained structures of wood, and some of these holes may have served as post-holes. Any wood, of course, rotted away centuries ago.

Modern visitors are often astounded by the towering stones. They can hardly believe that men armed only with ropes and levers could possibly have set them up. But this would have been nowhere near as hard as getting the stones to Stonehenge.

To raise the stones the first step was to dig a hole into which the base of the upright would fit. Then ropes would be attached to the upper end, and then perhaps 150 or 200 men would begin to pull. Slowly one end of the upright would be raised off the ground while the other slid into the hole. Stones or logs would be used to brace the upright, so that the pulling men could ease up without the stone falling to the ground again.

There are at least two methods by which the lintels could have been put on top of the uprights. First a ramp of earth might have been built up alongside the uprights, and the lintels simply dragged up. Another possibility is that they were raised on platforms. A low platform of logs would be built and the lintel levered onto it. Next to it a slightly higher platform would be built and the lintel levered onto that. Then the first platform would be built up slightly higher, and so on, until by slow stages the lintel was level with the top of the uprights.

Each upright ends in a little knob. These knobs fit into shallow depressions in the lintels. Carpenters today use the same sort of technique to make strong joints. They call it a mortise and tenon joint. The depressions were probably ground into the lintels after they were on top of the ramp or log tower. The builders could then see just exactly where to place them so they would fit with the knobs.

All in all, Stonehenge took the labor of thousands of men over a period of several centuries. Obviously, it meant a great deal

to those who built it.   But what did it mean?   What was it
used for?   While scientists generally agree on how Stonehenge
was built, there is no agreement at all on why it was built.

Before we get into that controversy, however, we must make
one important point.   Stonehenge is so famous that many
people do not know that there are many other monuments,
built during the same period, in the same region.

Just a few miles from Stonehenge is a stone circle called Ave-
bury.   It is even larger than Stonehenge, although it is not
nearly so complex.

Also nearby is Silbury Hill, an enormous artificial mound that
may have taken more man-hours of labor to build than it took to
build Stonehenge itself.   The region is also dotted with earthen
circles and mounds as well as tombs constructed from huge
stones.   Moreover, similar sorts of monuments are found in
different parts of the British Isles, and throughout Europe.

Thus while the purpose of Stonehenge is unknown to us, it
is not an isolated mystery.   The prehistoric peoples of the British Isles and Western Europe built a large number of megalithic monuments.

But Stonehenge is unique in at least one respect.   The stones
are smoothed out, whereas in most other megalithic monuments
only rough stones are used.   The stonework at Stonehenge has
reminded some scientists of the stonework of the Mycenaeans, a
Bronze Age people who lived in Greece at about the time that
Stonehenge was being built.   The carving of a dagger found
inscribed in one of the Stonehenge megaliths also looks like a
type of dagger used by the Mycenaeans.   This has led to a
theory that the Mycenaeans—who were great travelers—may
somehow have supervised the construction of Stonehenge.

Now we are ready to tackle the question of what Stonehenge

was used for. Most scientists believe that it was some sort of temple. No one is sure what sort of worship went on there because we know nothing of the religion of the Wessex people. But it seems to have had something to do with the sun. Many primitive religions involve worship of the sun.

If you stand in the center of Stonehenge at dawn on Midsummer's Day—the longest day of the year—and look out toward the Avenue, you will see the sun rise almost directly above the Heel Stone. Thus the priests could have used Stonehenge for celebrating the summer solstice.

A few years ago an astronomer named Gerald Hawkins proposed that the priests of Stonehenge could have used the monument for many other astronomical calculations. By standing in the middle of Stonehenge and looking out through the narrow gate of the trilithons or over some of the other stones they could accurately gauge the position of the sun, the moon or some bright stars. Since the position of the astronomical bodies changes according to the time of year, the priests could mark the passage of time with a great deal of accuracy. By moving stones around in the Aubrey Holes, Hawkins said the priests could predict the years in which eclipses would occur. This would give them tremendous power since primitive people are usually very frightened of eclipses.

While most scientists agree that the midsummer's sunrise was marked at Stonehenge, they do not agree with the rest of Hawkins' theories. They say we just do not know enough about how Stonehenge really looked when it was in use.

So the controversy over Stonehenge continues. It will probably always be surrounded with an air of mystery, since its builders could leave no record of their intentions. But years of patient scientific investigation have cleared away some of the clouds. We now know, at least in a general way, who built Stonehenge, and how, even if we do not know why.

V
THE NAZCA DRAWINGS

No ONE KNOWS who first discovered the huge drawings in South America's coastal desert. Travelers walking through the drab and inhospitable region would have noticed strange "lines" in the sand. But they could make nothing of these lines.

When airplanes began to fly regularly over the coastal desert the pilots noticed that the desert floor seemed to be covered with huge drawings. Some were geometric figures like rectangles and squares. More fantastic were the figures of birds, spiders, monkeys, whales and a host of strange-looking creatures that it has been impossible to identify. There were also straight lines that ran for hundreds of yards, but seemed to begin and end nowhere. It looked almost as though a giant had been carelessly doodling on the desert floor.

The "lines" that had been seen by people on the ground were a part of these drawings. The drawings themselves were so huge that their true shape could not be made out from the surface. Thus the existence of the drawings had gone unnoticed for centuries.

These colossal drawings are located in the desert some 250 miles south of Lima, the capital of Peru. They are scattered over an area about sixty miles long and between five and ten miles wide. Most of the drawings are found on plateaus between two valleys, the Ica and the Nazca. Practically every flat spot in this region contains some sort of drawing.

Before we can discuss who made these drawings, why and

how, we have to take a closer look at the place in which they are located. The desert runs for some 2,000 miles along the coast of South America. It covers much of the coastline of Peru. It is quite narrow, varying in width between one and twenty-five miles. The desert, made up of high plains and low hills, rolls back from the coast of the Pacific Ocean. The great chain of the Andes mountains rise steeply from its western edge.

A unique set of geographical circumstances has created this desert. A cold ocean current flows along part of the South American coast. The current is like an icy river cutting through the tropical waters of the Pacific. It effectively blocks rain from falling along the coast. Only when the moist ocean air is pushed up over the mountains is it able to dump its accumulated moisture as rainfall. The Western slopes of the Andes which face away from the ocean are covered with a lush tropical rain forest. But on the coast is the desert, in which it almost never rains.

For much of the year this desert is cloudless and extremely hot. One traveler noted that it was "hot enough to boil your brains." Between May and November the cold current in the Pacific runs even colder. This creates a fog which often shrouds the desert. But still no rain falls.

It is because it almost never rains in this desert that the lines and drawings have survived at all, for they are quite fragile. The actual construction of the lines and figures was simple.

The floor of the desert is covered by a layer of dark rocks and pebbles. To make the lines the surface pebbles were removed to expose the lighter rocks and soil beneath them. The surface material was then piled in a uniform way on both sides of the line. From the air the figures and lines might seem etched by a light colored line, which itself is outlined by two darker filaments. When the sun is low the little piles of pebbles cast long shadows which make the outlines of the drawings clearer.

If there were heavy rains on the Peruvian coast these figures would have been washed away centuries ago. But scientists have estimated that they have lasted for some 1,500 years already.

The rocks and pebbles on the surface of the desert are dark in color because they contain iron. This iron oxidizes and turns dark on contact with the air. The longer the iron-bearing rocks are exposed to the air, the darker they will get. People sometimes say that such rocks have received a coat of "desert varnish." The rocks oxidize and darken very slowly. But those stones that were artificially exposed to make up the lines and figures are darker and much harder to see than they were at first. One day the lines will fade out entirely.

Some people have said that these lines are "Inca roads." The region in which they lie was at one time part of the great Inca Empire. But they are not roads at all because they do not lead anywhere, and they were made centuries before the Incas ever appeared in Peru. In fact, an Inca road runs right through some of the figures. The Incas apparently were not interested in them. The descendants of the people who made the lines were probably subjects of the Incas.

The Spanish conquistadors under Francisco Pizarro conquered the Incas in 1533. But the Spanish also were uninterested in the figures in the desert. Early Spanish records contain no mention of them. The only people who might have known about the lines and figures were the people who lived in the region. But they were all killed off in the terrible wars that followed Pizarro's conquest.

So we only know in a general way who built the lines and when. We say that they are at least 1,500 years old. Scientists got that date through a lucky accident. At the end of one of the lines they found an old tree stump. No trees grow in this region so the stump obviously was brought there. Its placement at the very end of a line made scientists believe that the line builders used it as some sort of marker when they were making the lines.

The age of a piece of wood can be determined by a technique called radio-carbon dating. Just how this works is too complicated to go into here. For us the important thing to know is that the tests indicated the tree had been cut 1,500 years ago, probably while the lines were being built. An age of 1,500 years also fits in with other things that we know about the people who lived on the fringes of the desert.

About 2,000 years ago a number of peoples flourished near the desert. They lived mostly in the valleys on the desert's eastern side. These valleys were formed by rivers and streams carrying water down to the sea from the torrential storms that drench the rain forests on the other side of the Andes. The water deposits fertile silt in the valleys. By employing painstakingly careful methods of irrigation, crops can be grown in these valleys.

Racially and culturally all the people who settled in these desert valleys came from the same basic stock. But the valleys were separated from one another by long stretches of desert, so people did not go back and forth too often. As a result each region developed its own individual way of life.

In the northern valleys were a people we call the Mochicas. They were experts at making pottery. In the center valleys were the Paracas, who were superbly skilled at embroidery and weaving. In the South between the Ica and the Nazca valleys were the people scientists call the Ica-Nazcas. They made excellent pottery and fabrics, but they are now most well-known for the lines and figures they made in the desert. Some of the designs found in their pottery and weaving have been repeated on a gigantic scale in the desert figures.

As we have seen, the lines and figures themselves were fairly easy to etch into the surface of the desert. But first the figures would have to have been drawn as scale models, then traced in final form on the desert floor. So the moving and piling of all those rocks and stones, not to mention the time that it took to lay out the figures in the first place, must have involved thousands of man-hours of work in the broiling sun.

These figures must have been important to those who made them. They were important enough for the Ica-Nazca people to take a large number of laborers away from the hard job of growing food and send them into the desert to create these giant figures. What could their significance have been?

An interesting, but controversial, theory was advanced by Dr. Paul Kosok, a historian from Long Island University. Dr. Kosok was studying the peoples of ancient Peru. He and his wife went to Peru in 1941. On June 22 the couple happened to be in the desert looking at the lines and figures. In the southern hemisphere, June 22 is the day of the winter solstice, the shortest day of the year. Dr. Kosok and his wife followed one of the lines up a small mesa. As they stood pondering the significance of the lines the sun began to set.

To their surprise the setting sun touched the horizon right over one of the lines at whose base they stood. Quite suddenly Dr. Kosok had an inspiration that these lines were part of a gigantic system of astronomical calculation. Later he wrote, "the largest astronomy book in the world seemed spread out before us."

He assumed that if the Ica-Nazca priests stood at certain spots on the lines and watched where the sun set or rose they would be able to tell what time of the year it was, just as he and his wife had seen the sun set right over a particular line on the shortest day of the year.

Dr. Kosok was pressed for time, and he had to leave Peru before he could do much work on his theory. He had always planned to return to continue his work, and he did so briefly years later. But he died long before his project was completed. Others have taken up this theory and attempted to work it out more exactly.

Some of the things that we know about the civilizations of ancient Peru make the desert calendar theory attractive. First the ancient Peruvians were farmers, so exact knowledge of the change of seasons would have been important to them. Still they would not have needed such an elaborate method of telling the seasons to know when the proper planting time was.

Another possible reason for building a vast desert calendar was that the Ica-Nazca people probably lived in a theocracy— a society that was ruled by priests. In most South American Indian civilizations the main duty of the priests was to study the movements of the sun, moon and stars. The Indians of South and Central America were fascinated by time. The date upon which an event took place was of paramount significance. The Indians developed a calendar that was better than any used by the more advanced civilizations of Europe and Asia. So if any people in the world were going to lavish a great deal of time and effort on building a great calendar the Indian civilizations of South America were the ones.

Not all of the scientists who have studied the lines and figures of the Nazca region agree that they were part of a desert calendar. They raise many of the same objections that were raised to a similar theory regarding Stonehenge.

No astronomical theories can possibly account for all of the tracings in the desert. Some of these lines may really have been the outlines of roads, or more accurately ceremonial avenues along which religious processions passed. The rectangles and some of the other geometric figures could have been sacred enclosures, in which the rituals of this deeply religious society were performed.

Most puzzling of all are the drawings of surrealistic spiders, whales, birds, monkeys and other figures. What could their purpose have been? Even if a man stands upon a high platform he can get only a partial glimpse of them. Usually he would be completely unable to make out what these figures were supposed to be. Only with the invention of the airplane have men been able to see the huge figures in their entirety.

Drawing of a monkey in the Nazca desert.

The probable answer is that the figures were not meant for the eyes of men. They were meant to be seen only by the gods of the Ica-Nazca people who lived in the sky.

VI
SACSAHUAMAN

PEDRO DE CIEZA DE LEON was a sixteenth-century Spanish soldier and historian. He came to the New World with the Spanish conquerors of Peru. Cieza de Leon was impressed by the civilization of the Incas who had ruled Peru before the coming of the Spanish. He was particularly struck by the enormous fortress which overlooked the Inca capital of Cuzco. He tried to compare it to the greatest works he knew from Europe, "neither the stone aqueduct of Segovia nor the buildings of Hercules, nor the work of the Romans had the dignity of this fortress. . . ." Here was a monument that seemed to surpass anything that European engineering had been able to produce.

In our history books the great fortress is called Sacsahuaman, "the speckled hawk." This is not quite correct. Sacsahuaman is really the name of the cliff on which the fortress stands. The Incas themselves called the fortress Intihusai, "the house of the sun." But since Sacsahuaman is the name now commonly in use we shall also use it.

Before we can understand how and why this mighty fortress was built, we must know a little of the Incas and of their great city of Cuzco. According to Inca legend the First Lord Inca and founder of the Inca Empire was named Manco Capac. He was said to have come to the valley of Cuzco in the mountains of Peru and built a city there. The legends do not say when Manco Capac lived, but archaeologists place the founding of Cuzco at about A.D. 1100.

In the centuries that followed the Incas began to conquer neighboring peoples and build a huge empire. By the year 1500 as much as one-third of the entire South American continent was under the control of the Incas.

The Incas were not innovators. They adapted the techniques of the peoples they conquered, but they did so on a grand scale, for they were superb organizers. The Incas built an elaborate system of roads to connect the widely scattered provinces of their empire. They also built many new cities. Being an orderly people the Incas did not allow their cities to simply spring up and grow any old way. All cities were carefully planned. Sometimes small models of buildings or portions of cities were made in clay before the actual construction was begun.

All Inca cities followed the general plan that was first used at Cuzco. Streets were laid out in a grid pattern, much like the streets of many modern cities. All the major streets led to a central square. Around the square were located the temples, the houses of the priests and the residence of the Inca king himself. (The Inca king is often referred to as the Lord Inca or simply as the Inca.)

Though they were a warrior people, who were almost always fighting somewhere, the Incas built no walled cities to protect themselves. They did not need them. Most major Inca cities were built close to hills. On these hills was a fortress the Incas called a *pucara*. In time of attack the people, or at least the members of the aristocracy and the soldiers could retreat to this *pucara* and conduct a defense from there. Many of the *pucaras* were minature cities in themselves. They were designed to withstand a long siege. Sacsahuaman was the *pucara* of the city of Cuzco.

In the year 1437 the eighth Lord Inca, Viracocha, was besieged within Cuzco by a hostile tribe. The following year

Viracocha's son drove the invaders out of Cuzco, and was proclaimed the ninth Lord Inca. He took the name Pachacuti, which means "Earthshaker."

Perhaps it was the shock that an enemy could actually invade the sacred precincts of Cuzco itself that caused Pachacuti to order the construction of Sacsahuaman. The man who first planned the fortress was named Hualkpa Rimachi Inca. Many consider him to be one of the master-builders of history.

The hill of Sacsahuaman rises steeply to a height of 600 feet above the city of Cuzco. From the South, the side facing the city, the fortress at the top was virtually unreachable. One narraw path led to it and this could be easily blocked. Yet even here, where elaborate defenses would seem unnecessary, the fortress was surrounded by a massive wall. On the northern side where an attack would have been much easier, the Incas built a wall of incredible strength. The northern wall is fifteen hundred feet long. It is composed of three tiers or terraces, each standing a little higher than the next.

Inside the fortress stood three towers. One of them, called the Round Tower, was in reality a palace for the king. He could and probably did hold court there even if Cuzco itself was not under threat. The tower contained accommodations for the Inca's many wives, a royal bath, storerooms for the treasures of Cuzco and provisions for all the luxuries of life, even a brewery.

The other two towers of Sacsahuaman were taller but simpler. They were square and housed the troops who formed a permanent garrison for the fortress. The purpose of these towers was purely military. All the towers were connected by underground passages. The fortress itself could have held as many as ten thousand inhabitants during a siege. Since it had its own water supply and was well stocked with both food and weapons, Sacsahuaman could have been effectively defended for many months even if completely cut off from outside help.

The Incas were master stoneworkers. They used many different techniques for building. In some of their structures they used square stones cut like bricks. The stones in the walls of Sacsahuaman are irregular in shape, yet they fit together perfectly. They are arranged a little like the pieces of a jigsaw puzzle. This interlocking of the stones makes the entire wall stronger, for there was no mortar used in the walls. The stones themselves are enormous. Some of the larger ones weigh nearly two hundred tons.

Inca workmen quarried and shaped their stones in much the same way that other ancient peoples did. Usually they searched for natural cracks in the cliffs. These would be widened by forcing in wooden wedges and soaking them with water, or by building fires and then dousing them with cold water. When an appropriately sized boulder was cracked from the cliff it would then be hammered roughly into shape with stone tools. The Incas did use some metal tools but most stone-working was done with stone tools.

The rough stones were then dragged by teams of men up to the site. The quarries for the fortress were quite nearby, so that the stones of Sacsahuaman did not have to be dragged for a great distance. For the first layer of stones on the wall a deep hole was dug and very large stones levered and pushed into it, so that the foundation would be secure. After the first row of stones was laid, ramps were built alongside it so that the upper layers of stones could be dragged into place.

The most puzzling feature of the walls of Sacsahuaman was how the Inca engineers got the irregularly sized stones to fit so perfectly into one another. The Spanish observed that not even a knife-blade could be inserted between them. Some believe

Inca stone masons at work.

that the stones were dragged up on their ramps to see how they would fit. They would then be hauled down, shaped a bit more and once again dragged up and tested for fit. This process might have to be repeated a hundred times before the stonemasons made a perfect fit. Others who have examined the walls of Sacsahuaman think that the constant lifting and taking down of stones weighing many tons would have been both impossible and unnecessary. They think the Incas measured out the shape of the stone they would need, made a pattern of it and then shaped the stone to the size of the pattern. But we really have no way of knowing exactly what system the Incas used.

The Spaniards asked the Incas how the wonderful stone-fitting had been accomplished. They were told the stones were "softened" and made easier to shape by the application of the juice of certain red leaves. There are some chemical agents that can "soften" stones and make them easier to work, but there is no evidence that the Incas ever used any of them. Most experts think that the shaping was done by the use of simple stone tools and a great deal of time and effort. The experts believe that the Incas were just telling the Spaniards a bit of magical folklore about "softening" the stones.

As with the pyramids and most other ancient monuments, the "secret" of the builders lay in their ability to organize the labor of thousands of men effectively. The Incas told their Spanish conquerors that twenty thousand men had labored on the fortress and that the work had continued on and off for nearly seventy years. Indeed, the fortress was not really entirely completed when the Inca Empire fell in 1533 to the Spanish under Francisco Pizarro.

Pizarro's men captured Atahualpa, the Lord Inca, outside of Cuzco, so he never had a chance to use his great fortress against the invaders. Pizarro only had a tiny army and a few pieces of artillery and he faced tens of thousands of Inca warriors. Yet Inca society was so structured that the capture (and ultimate murder) of the Inca king put the Inca Empire in a virtual state of shock. Historians have often debated the reasons why the great Inca Empire seemed to crumble so quickly.

Whatever the reasons, by the time the Incas recovered sufficiently to offer effective resistance to the Spaniards, the invaders were already in complete control of Cuzco.

Most of the buildings of Cuzco were simple structures of wood. These were quickly destroyed. The Spanish then started to build their own city atop the ruins of the Incas' Cuzco. They used the fortress of Sacsahuaman as a stone quarry for their own buildings. The damage they did was so great that in a mere eight years after their capture of Cuzco, the Spanish commander of the city was forced to outlaw further raids on Sacsahuaman for stone. He feared that soon nothing would be left of the great fortress.   The order was never completely obeyed and for centuries treasure hunters and vandals continued to ravage the fortress.   Today only the great walls are left to remind the world of the power and glory of the Incas.

The valley in which Cuzco is nestled, like much of Peru, is subject to violent earthquakes.   The buildings of the Spanish at Cuzco have almost all been destroyed through the centuries. But the walls of Sacsahuaman remain.   One of the early Spanish conquerors said of the fortress, "To set the base they [the Incas] excavated down to the very rock, this they did so well that the foundation will remain as long as the world shall last."

VII
THE EASTER ISLAND STATUES

ON EASTER SUNDAY, 1772 A DUTCH SHIP, the *Arena,* landed at
an island that was not on any map.   The commander of the
Arena named the island in honor of the day.   He called it
Easter Island.

Look at a large map that shows the Pacific Ocean, and try
to find Easter Island.   First locate Chile on the West coast of
South America.   Now go down Chile about one-third of the way
and start looking West, out into the Pacific Ocean.   Keep looking, and you will find Easter Island, but it is a long way, even on
a map.   Actually Easter Island is two thousand miles from the
coast of Chile.   The nearest inhabited island is twelve hundred
miles away.   As you can see, Easter Island is pretty isolated.
It could almost be called the most isolated spot on earth.   That
is why the sailors did not discover it until 1772.

From the sea, Easter Island looks forbidding.   It is dominated
by a huge extinct volcano.   The island is shaped like a triangle
and there is a huge extinct volcano near each point of this triangle.   So no matter which side you approach the island from,
it looks pretty much the same.

The men of the *Arena* were surprised to find the island was
inhabited.   The natives of Easter Island were a familiar type to
the sailors.   They were Polynesians, a tall, sturdy, brown-skinned
people who lived on many of the islands of the South Pacific.
But Easter Island was so remote that the people there had no
contact with people who lived on the other Polynesian islands.

The Easter Island natives greeted the Dutch ship enthusiastically. They swam out to where it was anchored. When ropes and ladders were thrown over to them they did not hesitate a moment before climbing aboard. Once aboard they ran all over this ship, exploring everything. All the while they were laughing and shouting, obviously in high good humor. The reserved Dutch sailors did not know what to make of this strange behavior.

Soon the Easter Islanders began to act even more strangely. They started stealing things like the sailors' caps. One of the natives even stole the Admiral's tablecloth and gleefully jumped overboard before anyone could stop him.

To the people of Easter Island there was nothing unusual or unfriendly about stealing. For them the idea of private property did not exist. If a person wanted something, he took it. No one got angry, no one thought of this as stealing. But the upright Dutch sailors could not understand what was happening. They became very angry and nervous.

When a landing party from the *Arena* rowed ashore all the sailors carried loaded guns. The natives on the beach were behaving even more strangely than they had on the boat. Some looked very friendly. Others did not look friendly at all and a few began throwing rocks at the sailors.

Then one of the sailors panicked and shouted the order to open fire. In the next few seconds several of the natives were killed and the rest ran away.

The Dutch knew they were wrong. But there was really nothing more they could do, so they left quickly.

During their brief stay on the island the Dutch sailors had caught a glimpse of some enormous statues. They saw numerous figures of men with long, oversized heads. Admiral Roggeveen wrote, "These stone figures filled us with amazement, for we could not understand how people without solid spars

[wooden posts] and without ropes were able to raise them. . . ."

The years after 1772 were tragic ones for the people of Easter Island. Thousands lived on the island. They were divided into tribes, and the tribes often fought one another. For some unknown reason the wars between the tribes were unusually severe in the years around 1772. The wars disrupted life on the island so badly that people no longer had time to build their great statues. What is more, most of the statues that had been set up were pushed over and broken during the conflict.

Worse events were to come. In 1862 a slave ship from South America carried off a thousand people from the island. This brutal slave raid shocked many of the missionaries of the South Pacific. They appealed to different world governments to have the captives returned. The appeal finally succeeded, but it was too late, for only fifteen of the original thousand captives were still alive. All the others had died from hardship and disease. Even the fifteen survivors had contracted the deadly disease smallpox. When they were returned to Easter Island they spread the disease among their fellow islanders.

At the best of times six thousand people may have lived on Easter Island. In the 1880s the population was down to 111. Today the population has risen to several hundred, and the people no longer live in complete poverty.

It was not until the last fifty or sixty years that the outside world began to take an interest in Easter Island. Adventurers and scientists began to visit the island. Today there are regular tourist flights to Easter Island. Everyone who visits the island wants to see the great statues. Some of the fallen statues have been set up again. They are as awe-inspiring to the modern visitor as they were to Admiral Roggeveen back in 1772. No one can look at them without wondering how they were built.

There is no mystery about how the statues were carved.

Most of them were cut from the rock of the volcano Rano Raraku. A quarry on the slopes of the volcano still contains some two hundred unfinished statues. These statues were cut right out of the side of the volcano.

An anthropologist who visited the island in the 1930s described the quarry this way:

"To the visitor walking around the quarry it seems as though this were a day of rest. The workmen have gone home to their villages but tomorrow they will be back. . . . How could they fail to come back, these sculptors who have left their tools lying at the foot of the work, where one only has to bend down to pick them up."

The tools were the simplest kind—pointed hard stones. Volcanic rock is not the hardest rock in the world, but it is hard enough. Carving one of the great statues out of the rock with stone tools took a long time and a lot of hard work.

Modern Easter Islanders have attempted to carve the stone in the volcano with the same kind of tools that their ancestors used. If a team of a dozen men worked sixteen hours a day it would take them about a year to carve a fifteen-foot statue. The stone-carvers of olden times were undoubtedly more skilled than the modern islanders, so they could probably have done the job in a little less time. But carving one of the giant statues of Easter Island was a giant-sized job. And carving the statues was just the beginning. After that it had to be moved.

No one knows exactly how many statues were originally scattered around the island, but there were many hundreds of them.

The largest completed statue is thirty-three feet high and weighs ninety tons. A much larger statue that would have stood sixty-six feet high, if it had been completed, is still half-finished in the quarry.

Most of the Easter Island statues were used as part of a burial ceremony. They were set up around the area in which the body of the dead man was placed. The religion of the Easter Islanders required that the burial enclosures be built along the coast. This meant that some of the great statues had to be moved as much as ten miles from the volcano to the coast.

The Easter Islanders had no horses to do the pulling for them. In fact, there were no large animals of any kind on the island. The men supplied all the power. They did not know how to use the wheel. Even if they had known how to build carts to load the statues on there would not have been enough wood to build them. Very few trees grow on Easter Island and wood is extremely scarce. And even if they had built carts, the carts would have been useless. The surface of the island is covered with boulders. Walking is hard enough. Pulling a wheeled cart with a twenty- or thirty-ton statue in it would have been impossible.

In 1955 the Norwegian anthropologist Thor Heyerdahl went to Easter Island. He wanted to find out how the statues had been moved. He gathered a crew of 180 natives. The men made ropes from reeds that grow on the island. They then tied the ropes to a twelve-ton statue and began to pull. After a few pulls they were able to move the statue quite easily.

Heyerdahl wrote, "We had established that 180 natives . . . could draw a twelve-ton statue across the plain, and if we had many more people, we could have drawn a much larger figure."

The next big job was setting the statue upright. How were the Easter Islanders, without machinery, able to lift such an enormous weight?

Again Heyerdahl turned to the natives of the island and asked them how they would do it. One old man, Pedro Atan, who was called the "mayor" of the island, said that his grandfather had told him how the statues had been set up. For $100 he agreed to demonstrate how it was done. When the statues were first set up the workmen were probably paid in food by the family of the man whose burial enclosure was being built.

"Mayor" Pedro Atan gathered a crew of eleven relatives and friends. They found a large fallen statue and pushed long poles under it. Using the poles as levers they managed to raise first one end of the statue and then the other a few inches off the ground. The mayor quickly shoved stones under the raised portion. With each lift they managed to raise the statue just a little more. Slowly the pile of stones under the figure grew. The men began putting more stones under the head and shoulders of the statue.

After eighteen days the statue rested on top of a diagonal pile of stones. Then the men tied ropes around the statue's forehead. With a few good tugs they were able to haul it into

Raising an Easter Island statue.

an upright position.   (The megaliths of Stonehenge were raised in much the same way.)

A final mystery about the construction of the Easter Island statues remained.   When they had first been set up each had what looked like a red hat.   These "hats" were cylinders of red volcanic rock, placed atop the statue's head.   They were not meant to represent hats.   In the old days the men of Easter Island wore long hair which they tied into a knot on the top of their head.   The red "hat" represented this hair style.

These "hats" might weigh up to ten tons.   How could they be lifted on top of a thirty-foot statue?   The obvious way would have been to build a pile of stones under the "hat" in the same way as the stones were built up under the statue itself.   The "hat" could be raised to the level of the statue's head, and then pushed over and placed on top of it.

The mayor offered to show Heyerdahl how it was done, but the project was never carried through.

After Heyerdahl discovered what the natives of Easter Island can do today, there was no longer any mystery abut how the Easter Island monuments were built.   We have to remember that while the people of Easter Island were building their great statues, the population of the island may have been as high as six thousand.   There was plenty of food available and no one had to work very hard to get enough to eat.   The island was small and so isolated that people had nowhere to go.   So when there were no wars, the people of Easter Island had a lot of time to spend on building their great monuments.   They built their statues so well that they still amaze us today.

VIII
GREAT ZIMBABWE

ON SEPTEMBER 5, 1871 a German explorer named Karl Gottlieb Mauch climbed a hill in southern Africa and gazed down upon an amazing sight. Spread out beneath him was what seemed to be a city of stone. Mauch knew that he had found the place called Zimbabwe, of which he had heard so much.

When Mauch reached Zimbabwe it was deserted save for one old man who claimed to be a high priest of Zimbabwe. Mauch could not understand what the old man was trying to tell him. He was also thoroughly puzzled by the appearance of Zimbabwe itself. He believed that there was nothing else like it in all Africa.

Mauch finally made his way back to Germany and wrote a book about his travels in Africa. In the book he speculated about who had built Zimbabwe and why. When a man is confronted with something unknown he often tries to relate it to something that he knows. Mauch attempted to do this with Zimbabwe. He really knew very little about it so he tried to link it up with something he knew very well—the Bible.

In the Bible there is the story of how King Solomon sent ships to a place called Ophir to obtain gold. Ophir was commonly called the location of "King Solomon's Mines." But the Bible gave very little information about the location of Ophir, so no one knew where it was. Practically every place that was known to have gold was, at one time or another, identified as the land of Ophir. In fact, we are still not sure where Ophir was. But Karl Mauch was sure that Ophir was the place called Zimbabwe because many gold mines were rumored to be in the Zimbabwe

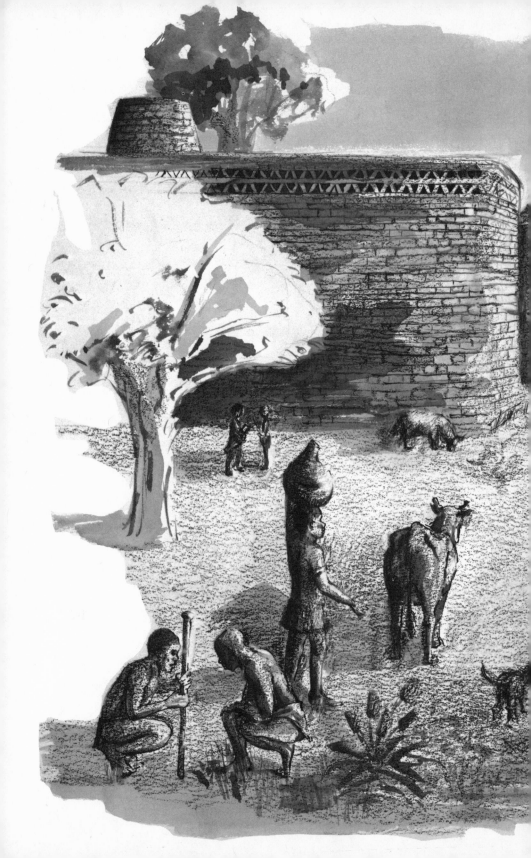

region.   Mauch even went so far as to say that the stone structures had been built by the Queen of Sheba's workmen in imitation of King Solomon's palace.

Mauch's theory was wrong.   So were the theories proposed by a lot of other Europeans who visited Zimbabwe.   Even today there is a certain amount of mystery about Zimbabwe.   It is not that we do not know who built Zimbabwe.   We do.   It was built by a series of black African peoples who lived in the region and whose descendants still live there.   The confusion about Zimbabwe developed because a lot of white people refused to believe that black Africans could construct such an imposing monument.   The confusion is particularly great because Zimbabwe is located in what is now the country of Rhodesia.   In that country a small white minority is attempting to retain all power at the expense of a large black majority.   In order to do this it is important for the white Rhodesian to believe that the black man is inferior and could not build such a monument.

But Zimbabwe is not really unique in Africa.   There are a number of stone monuments in the Central African plains called *dzimbabwe* or "great stone house."   The term is applied to any stone structure in which a king once held court.   The particular place that concerns us is called Great Zimbabwe because it is much larger than any other *dzimbabwe*.

Great Zimbabwe is located about halfway between two major African rivers, the Zambezi and the Limpopo.   It is about 150 miles from the West coast of the continent.   The area around it is a broad rolling valley that is occasionally broken by steep and fantastically shaped cliffs.   Great Zimbabwe is partially located on one of these cliffs and it spreads out in the valley below.

There are several separate parts to Great Zimbabwe.   On the top of the hill is a structure that explorers have called the Acropolis.   Acropolis is a Greek word meaning a high and fortified part of a city. It is an appropriate label for this part of Zimbabwe. The Acropolis has thick walls and narrow passages. It overlooks a sheer ninety-foot drop, and can be reached only by means of a narrow and difficult trail. It is quite clearly a spot built for defense. When under attack the people of the valley could climb to the Acropolis. The trail to the top could then be blocked and the defenders would be able to hold out as long as they had enough food and water. The attackers, who would have been armed only with spears, would have no way of harming those inside the Acropolis.

The uses of the structures scattered throughout the valley are not so obvious. On a low hill about a quarter of a mile from the Acropolis is a walled structure that has been called the Temple or the Elliptical Building. The curved wall encloses an area roughly the length of a football field and about two-thirds as

Ruins of Zimbabwe seen from the air.

wide.   The wall itself is up to thirty feet high and fifteen feet thick.   Inside this main wall are a number of other walls all roughly circular or oval in shape.   Also inside the wall is a thirty-foot-high rounded tower called the Conical Tower.   The remains of another tower have been found next to the Conical Tower.

Between the Temple and the Acropolis are the ruins of a number of smaller stone structures that seem to reproduce, in miniature, the features found in the Temple.

All of Great Zimbabwe is built by a technique called dry stone masonry.   Basically this is a very simple way of building things with stone.   One flat stone is piled on top of another.   No mortar is used to hold the stones in place.   In many parts of the United States farmers built, and still build, dry stone walls and fences.   But building a dry stone wall a few feet high, and piling one thirty feet high, are two very different jobs.   The builder of the high wall must be extremely skillful and observe certain rules.

All the high walls at Zimbabwe have a pronounced batter, that is they are narrower at the top than at the bottom.   This wide base makes the pile of stones more stable.   There are no straight stretches of wall at Zimbabwe.   All the walls curve at least slightly.   The curve also gives dry stone walls greater strength.

This particular sort of construction was probably inevitable in the Zimbabwe region because of the nature of the available building materials.   The rock around Zimbabwe is all granite.   When granite is exposed to the weather it may break off in a process called exfoliation.   That is, chunks tend to peel away in layers, a little like the way that layers can be peeled off an onion.   With a few sharp taps a man can convert one of these shell-like layers of granite into a nicely shaped flat stone, suitable for piling.

The builders of Great Zimbabwe undoubtedly ran out of natural bricks long before their monument was finished. But they could get more material by quarrying stones with fire and wedges. There are many people in Africa today who are still quite expert at the techniques of dry stonemasonry.

Great Zimbabwe is not nearly as old as the first European explorers thought it was. Nor were its builders any exotic immigrants from the land of the Queen of Sheba. Construction of Great Zimbabwe began a little over a thousand years ago. That is a long time, but Solomon and Sheba lived nearly three thousand years ago. We cannot exactly name those who first started building Great Zimbabwe, but we do know that they were a Bantu people. Bantu is a general term that describes a large and varied group of Negroid peoples who spread throughout much of central and southern Africa during the last two thousand years.

The Zimbabwe region was inhabited a long time before the coming of the Bantus. Back around the time Solomon and Sheba lived, the hill and valley on which Great Zimbabwe now stands was the home of cattle-raising nomads who possessed a neolithic culture. About two thousand years ago gold mining operations began in the region. The miners first worked only those veins which were near the surface. As the surface veins were exhausted the miners were forced to improve their technique so they could dig deeper. We are not sure how much gold the Zimbabwe region yielded, for most of it was dug out centuries ago. But it seems fairly certain that the region was never as fabulously rich in gold as later seekers for "King Solomon's Mines" imagined it to be.

The Bantus arrived somewhere around A.D. 1000. They too were a cattle-raising people, but considerably more technically advanced than the previous inhabitants of the Zimbabwe region.

For example, the Bantus knew how to make iron tools and weapons. It was these Bantu peoples then, who first began to put up the stone walls of Zimbabwe.

Once we realize that the cattle-raising Bantus built Zimbabwe, the function of the so-called Temple becomes clear. It is not a temple at all but a large stone replica of a typical Bantu structure called a kraal. The kraal is an enclosure in which a Bantu family lives. It is a walled area, inside of which are the huts for the family and a place to keep the cattle. Kraals are usually built of wood, mud, leaves and other perishable materials.

Among the early Bantus, the king held a very high position. He was believed to have god-like powers. Powerful Bantu monarchs often had large and elaborate kraals built for themselves. Great Zimbabwe is the largest of these. It was meant to house the king and his numerous wives, as well as high officials in the royal court. The high walls were not for physical protection. There were too many doorways which could not be easily defended. If an attack came the king would flee to the Acropolis. Rather the walls were to shield the sacred person of the king from the profane gaze of the common people.

Great Zimbabwe with its fortress and stone kraal became the headquarters for a succession of Bantu kingdoms. Since the Bantus had no written language there are no records to accurately trace the waxing and waning of the power of the early kings of Zimbabwe. Around the year 1500 the Portuguese established trading posts along the East coast of Africa. One of their major ports was Sofala which is almost due East of Great Zimbabwe. The Portuguese themselves never ventured inland to see Great Zimbabwe, but gold from the kings who ruled there was brought to them by Arab traders or occasionally by stately, leopard-skin draped, black warriors. In return the people of Great Zimbabwe received a wide variety of goods from Europe and Asia. Archaeologists at Zimbabwe have found everything from Chinese pots to a sixteenth-century liquor bottle from Holland.

Just before the arrival of the Portuguese the kings of Zimbabwe had experienced a brief golden age. Under the leadership of some exceptionally able kings they had carved out the largest native empire in Africa. These kings collected tribute from such a wide area that they had earned themselves the name of *Mwena Mutapa*, or "Master Pillager." The name was one of praise rather than an insult, and the kings themselves used it frequently. The Portuguese did not understand the name and thought that the empire was ruled by a monarch named Monomotapa. During this period Great Zimbabwe was enlarged.

The kings of Great Zimbabwe were never able to establish a stable empire for very long. A strong ruler might be able to hold the tribes together for as long as he lived, but after his death the system collapsed, and his successor would have to try to start building the empire all over again.

Great Zimbabwe itself was the property first of one ruling group then another. Finally it ceased to be a home for kings at all. The rulers of the region moved their capital a hundred miles north to Manyanga. But because of its age and traditions, Great Zimbabwe continued to be regarded as an important religious center.

Great Zimbabwe ceased to be of any importance at all during the early years of the nineteenth century. Its end came swiftly and dramatically. Well to the south of Zimbabwe the great Zulu empire was beginning to expand. All those tribes which did not submit were forced to flee before the invincible Zulu army. Among the refugees were the Ngoni tribe who were themselves a fierce warrior people. The Ngoni invaded the land of the kings of Zimbabwe, and in 1833 overran Great Zimbabwe itself.

All those who lived in or near the stone monument either

ran away or were slaughtered. The Ngoni had no use for Great Zimbabwe and soon abandoned it. A few of the former residents, mostly priests, crept back from hiding and tried to re-establish Great Zimbabwe as a place of worship once again. But it was no use. The ravages of the Ngoni had broken the back of the Zimbabwe culture.

So you can see it was not very long—a mere thirty-seven years —after Zimbabwe had been abandoned that Karl Mauch "discovered" it and began weaving fantasies around it. But some of the people who had helped to build Zimbabwe and who lived there were still very much alive. The old man Mauch found living among the ruins tried to tell him about Great Zimbabwe, but Mauch could not understand what the old man was saying. He could not believe that "natives," particularly black natives, could build such a place. A lot of other early explorers could not believe it either. But we now know, beyond a shadow of a doubt, that they did.

A SELECTED BIBLIOGRAPHY

The following books should be readily available and are suggested as further reading. Those marked with an asterisk (*) will be of particular interest to younger readers.

CHAPTER I—MONUMENTS THEN AND NOW
Ceram, C. W. *Gods, Graves and Scholars* (revised edition). New York: Alfred A. Knopf, 1967.
——. *The March of Archaeology*. New York: Alfred A. Knopf, 1958.
Cottrell, Leonard. *The Anvil of Civilization*. New York: The New American Library, 1957.
——. *Wonders of the World*. New York: Holt, Rinehart and Winston, 1959.
Cohen, Daniel. *Mysterious Places*. New York: Dodd, Mead & Co., 1969.
De Camp, L. Sprague. *The Ancient Engineers*. New York: Doubleday, 1963.
—— and de Camp, Catherine. *Ancient Ruins and Archaeology*. New York: Doubleday, 1964.
*National Geographic Society (editors). *Everyday Life in Ancient Times*. Washington, D.C.: The National Geographic Society, 1951.
Silverberg, Robert. *Empires in the Dust*. Philadelphia: Chilton, 1963.

CHAPTER II—THE TOWER OF BABEL
*Mellersh, H. E. L. *Sumer and Babylon*. New York: T. Y. Crowell, 1965.
Roux, George. *Ancient Iraq*. New York: World, 1964.

Saggs, H. W. F. *The Greatness that Was Babylon.* New York: Hawthorn, 1962.

CHAPTER III—THE PYRAMIDS
*Cormack, Maribelle. *Imhotep, Builder in Stone.* New York: Franklin Watts, 1965.
*Cohen, Daniel. *Secrets from Ancient Graves.* New York: Dodd, Mead & Co., 1968.
Cottrell, Leonard. *Life Under the Pharaohs.* New York: Holt, Rniehart & Winston, 1960.
——. *The Mountains of Pharaoh.* New York: Holt, Rinehart & Winston, 1956.
Edwards, I. E. S. *The Pyramids of Egypt.* Baltimore, Md.: Penguin Books, 1961.
Fakhry, Ahmed. *The Pyramids.* Chicago: The University of Chicago Press, 1961.

CHAPTER IV—STONEHENGE
*Branley, Franklyn. *The Mystery of Stonehenge.* New York: T. Y. Crowell, 1969.
Crampton, Patrick. *Stonehenge of the Kings.* New York: John Day, 1968.
Daniel, Glyn. *The Megalith Builders of Western Europe.* London: Penguin Books, 1968.
Hawkins, Gerald S. *Stonehenge Decoded.* New York: Doubleday, 1963.
Van Doren Stern, Philip. *Prehistoric Europe.* New York: W. W. Norton, 1969.

CHAPTER V—THE NAZCA DRAWINGS
Deuel, Leo (editor). *Conquistadors Without Swords.* New York: St. Martin's, 1967.

————. *Flights Into Yesterday*. New York: St. Martin's, 1969.
Von Hagen, V. W. *The Desert Kingdoms of Peru*. New York: New American Library, 1968.

CHAPTER VI—SACSAHUAMAN
Brundage, Burr Cartwright. *Empire of the Inca*. Norman, Oklahoma: University of Oklahoma Press, 1963.
————. *Lords of Cuzco*. Norman, Oklahoma: University of Oklahoma Press, 1967.
Von Hagen, V. W. *The Ancient Sun Kingdoms of the Americas*. New York: World, 1961.
*————. *The Incas*. New York: World, 1961.

CHAPTER VII—THE EASTER ISLAND STATUES
Heyerdahl, Thor. *Aku-Aku*. New York: Rand McNally, 1958.
Metraux, Alfred. Easter Island, A *Stone Age Civilization of the Pacific*. New York: Oxford University Press, 1957.
Suggs, Robert C. *Lords of the Blue Pacific*. Greenwich, Conn.: New York Graphic Society, 1962.

CHAPTER VIII—GREAT ZIMBABWE
Davidson, Basil. *The Lost Cities of Africa*. Boston: Little, Brown & Co., 1959.
Silverberg, Robert. *Frontiers in Archaeology*. Philadelphia: Chilton, 1965.
*Valahos, Olivia. *African Beginnings*. New York: Viking, 1967.

INDEX